FOOD

created by

theimaginary**body**

script by

Joel Horwood and Christopher Heimann

theimaginary**body**, 4a Petherton Road, London N5 2RD
Tel: +44 (0)20 7704 9904
Email: info@theimaginarybody.co.uk
Web: **www.theimaginarybody.co.uk**

Tour booking enquiries for Food
Contact Ric Watts on ric@theimaginarybody.co.uk

FOOD

by **the**imaginary**body** *received its world premiere on 3 August 2006 at the Traverse Theatre as part of the Edinburgh Festival.*

Created by	**the**imaginary**body**
Script by	Joel Horwood and Christopher Heimann

FRANK	Sean Campion
CHERRY	Vic Bryson
TOM	Jon Foster
GEORGE	Graham O'Mara
CORDELIA	Shereen Martineau

All other parts played by the company

Director	Christopher Heimann
Dramaturg	Ruth Little
Designer	Jon Bausor
Movement Director	Ann Yee

Lighting Design	Jon Clark
Sound Design	Matt Downing
Set Build	Kenny Easson
Production Assistant	Laura Tantum
Production Assistant	Angie Baul

Producer	Diene Petterle
Producer	Ric Watts
Marketing	Kate Walker
	ekatew@btinternet.com
Press	The Sarah Mitchell Partnership
	www.thesmp.com
Print / Web Design	Christoph Stolberg

Acknowledgements

The development of Food has been generously supported by New Greenham Arts, Peggy Ramsay Foundation, Young Vic Theatre Company, BAC, and Arts Council England.

Thanks to

The actors who have contributed towards the development of *Food* over the past year: Poppy Miller, Gregory Gudgeon, Niall Costigan, Ellie Piercy, Jane Guernier, and Carl Prekopp. The Peggy Ramsay Foundation, Royal Academy of Dramatic Arts, Paul Gready at the Institute of Commonwealth Studies, Suli Majithia at the Actors Centre, Mike Dalton at Pop-Up Theatre, Michel Roux Jr. and Nicolas Laridan at Le Gavroche London, Isaac McHale and Brett Graham at Ledbury London, Lindsay Stewart at Wildcard PR, Jon Hickman at Hightide Productions, Willy Russell, David Pugh Ltd, Kate McGrath, Tom Morris, Claire Newby, Amy Ball, Jenny Worton, Janet Hodgson, Jemima Lee and David Micklem at Arts Council England, David Hardcastle at Rubbaglove, Robbie and Elen Bowman at Living Pictures Productions, Martin Hunt at Tartan Silk, Karen Albrecht at Coutts, Bruno De Oliveira, Richard Trafford and Victoria McKellar at Paul Smith.

Special thanks to

Laura Collier and all the staff at the Traverse Theatre; Martin Sutherland at New Greenham Arts; Nick, Matt, Claire and all at Nick Hern Books; Sue Emmas, David Lan and everyone at the Young Vic Theatre; David Jubb, Harun Morrison and everyone at BAC; Christine Heimann-Bossert, Diethard Heimann, Reinhard Bestgen, Hedwig Bossert and Marion Stuckenberg, Victoria Ward and everyone at Sparknow Ltd.

theimaginarybody

is an award winning theatre and film company that produces devised visual theatre, narrative-driven drama and runs educational drama workshops. The company was set up in 2002 by co-artistic directors – German theatre director Christopher Heimann and Brazilian film maker Diene Petterle. The company is interested in creating theatre and film with a focus on playful visual styles.

The company's first show, *100*, was a critical success, winning a Fringe First award in Edinburgh in 2002. This was followed by a London run at the Soho Theatre and a world tour, including dates at the World Stage Festival in Toronto, Canada; the Kilkenny Arts Festival in Ireland; the Perth International Arts Festival; the Adelaide Festival of Art, in Australia; and the Curitiba Festival in Brazil. The script was published by Nick Hern Books, and so far *100* has been performed by eight other companies worldwide.

Food is theimaginarybody's second theatre show, and receives its world premiere at the Traverse Theatre during the 2006 Edinburgh Fringe Festival, prior to UK and international touring throughout 2007.

The company has also produced two short films. *The Last Client* (2004) won first prize at the Tehran International Film Festival, 1st prize at the Black Images film festival and was a runner-up in the Race in The Media Awards. It was selected by the British Council to represent the UK abroad. *Mr Thompson's Carnation* (2001) was first screened at Cannes, won the Short Circuits Award and was subsequently theatrically released by Zoo Cinemas in London. It has been screened at the 46th London International Film Festival, and the Sao Paulo, Berlin, Kiev Molodist and Tehran International Film Festivals.

theimaginarybody and its members have run workshops in a wide range of settings. Actor training includes Royal Academy of Dramatic Art, Guildhall School of Music and Drama, Mountview Theatre Academy and the Adelaide Festival in Australia. Educational workshops include the Gate Theatre, the Arcola Theatre, the Young Vic Schools Theatre Festival, BAC, and the Big Issue Foundation. Corporate work includes clients such as Orange Communications and Her Majesty's Revenue and Customs.

BIOGRAPHIES

Jon Bausor – *Designer*

Jon read Music as a choral scholar at Oxford University and Fine Art at Exeter College of Art before training on the Motley Theatre Design Course. He was a finalist in The Linbury Prize 2000.

Recent theatre credits include: *The Soldiers Tale* (Old Vic / New York); *Shrieks of Laughter* (Soho Theatre); The *Great Highway* (Gate Theatre); *Cymbeline* (Regents Park Open Air Theatre); *The Hoxton Story* (Red Room / site specific); *Frankenstein* (Derby Playhouse); *Bread and Butter* (Oxford Stage Company / Tricycle Theatre); *Carver* (Arcola Theatre); *The Last Waltz* season (Oxford Stage Company / Dumbfounded Theatre); *Melody, In the Bag* (Traverse Theatre); *The New Tenant, Interior, The Exception and the Rule, Winners, The Soul of Chien-Nu* (Young Vic); *Sanctuary, The Tempest* (National Theatre); *Twelfth Night* (Cambridge Arts Theatre); *The Taming of the Shrew* (Thelma Holt / Theatre Royal, Plymouth / No.1 Tour); *Switchback, Possible Worlds* (Tron Theatre, Glasgow). Forthcoming work includes new commissions for the Royal Opera House, Lyric Theatre and Filter and *Julius Caesar* for the Abbey Theatre, Dublin.

Recent dance credits include: *Snow White in Black* (Phoenix Dance Theatre / Sadler's Wells and tour); *Ghosts, Before the Tempest . . . , Sophie, Stateless, Asyla* (Linbury Theatre, Royal Opera House); *Mixtures* (Westminster Abbey / English National Ballet); *Non Exeunt* (George Piper Dances / Sadler's Wells).

Opera design includes: *The Knot Garden* (Klangbogen Festival, Vienna); *The Queen of Spades* (Edinburgh Festival Theatre); *Cosi Fan Tutte* (Handmade Opera); *King Arthur* (New Chamber Opera).

Vic Bryson – *Cherry*

Theatre includes: *Jane Eyre* (Shared Experience); *Beyond Midnight, The Smallest Person* (Trestle Theatre Company); *Losing It* (Soho Theatre); *Galileo, The Taming of the Shrew* (Jumped Up); *Abigail's Party* (New Ambassadors / Whitehall Theatre); *The Railway Children, Trying to Get Back Home* (New Perspectives); *Struck* (Lightning Ensemble); *The Importance of Being Earnest* (Tour de Force); *A Summer's Day* (Westcliff Palace); *The Bug* (Box Clever); *The Fire-Raisers* (Man Called Uncle); *Southern Comfort* (Cornish Theatre Collective); *The Millennium Party* (The Hag Project); *Odes & Gameshows* (Camden People's Theatre); *Wanting It All* (Fluxx); *The Revenger's Tragedy* (Rogues Company); *St Joan* (Timezone Theatre Company); *Bunsen Towers Mystery* (New Kinetic); *Sister Mary Sessions* (Derry Playhouse, Ridiculusmus);

Speaking in Tongues (Old Fire Station); *Adventures of Huckleberry Finn* (French National Tour).

Television includes: *Bodyguards, Kavanagh QC*. Film includes: *Prayer Beads, You Don't Know The Half Of It, Black Doves*.

Sean Campion – *Frank*

Theatre includes: *Phaedra, The Cosmonauts Last Message* (Donmar Warehouse); *The Quare Fellow* (Oxford Stage Company); *Mutabilite, Tarry Flynn* (National Theatre); *Mayhem* (Royal Exchange, Manchester); *Blackwater Angel* (Finborough Theatre); Winners / Interior (Young Vic); *Da, Observe the Sons of Ulster marching towards the Somme, The Importance of Being Earnest, The Silver Tassie, Big Maggie* (Abbey Theatre, Dublin); *Beauty in a Broken Place, Good Evening Mr. Collins* (Peacock Theatre, Dublin); *Stones in His Pockets* – nominated for Olivier and Tony award for Best Actor (West End / Broadway); *Waiting for Godot* (Lyric Theatre,Belfast); *Northern Star* (Tinderbox Theatre); *The Mayor of Casterbridge* (Storytellers Theatre Company, Dublin); *Miss Julie* (Everyman Palace); *Equus, Bent* (Red Kettle Theatre Co. Ireland); *A Moon for the Misbegotten* (Dubbeljoint Theatre Company).

Television includes: *EastEnders, Holby, Fair City, Echoes*. Film includes: *Blackwater Lightship, Timbuktu, Goldfish Memory*.

Jon Clark – *Lighting Designer*

Jon studied Theatre Design at Bretton Hall.

Recent theatre credits include: *The Soldier's Tale* (The Old Vic, London); *Gone to Earth* (Shared Experience / Lyric Hammersmith & Tour); *The Tale That Wags The Dog* (Drum Theatre Plymouth, Skirball Center LA); *Underworld* (Frantic Assembly / Lyric Hammersmith & Tour); *Mandragora* (Tara Arts / Tron Theatre).

Recent lighting design for dance includes: *Real* (ACE Dance Company / UK Tour); *Mountains are Mountains* (Philipp Gehmacher / Tanz Quartier Vienna); *Into the Hoods* (ZooNation / Peacock Theatre); *Maverick Matador* (Juliet Aster Dance / Dance East); *Embryonic Dreams* (Pyromania / The Pleasance).

Recent lighting design for opera includes *L'Elisir D'Amore, The Barber of Seville, Cosi Fan Tutte* (Grange Park Opera).

Jon is Associate Lighting Designer for *Evita* at The Adelphi Theatre, London.

Matt Downing – *Sound Designer*

Matt Downing is a freelance sound designer, composer and music producer.

Recent theatre credits include: *Mariana Pineda, Gaudeamus* (Arcola Theatre); *Hiding, Blue Orange* (Watford Palace Theatre); *The Gigli Concert* (Assembly Rooms); *Year 10* (Théâtre National de Strasbourg); *After Haggerty, The Gabriels, Year 10, Hortensia, The Museum of Dreams, The Gigli Concert, Etta Jenks* (Finborough Theatre); *Hitting Town, The Revenger's Tragedy, The Canterville Ghost* (Southwark Playhouse); *Year 10* (BAC); *Scotch, Water / Ponies* (Hen and Chickens); *Twelfth Night* (tour, R.J. Williamson Company); *Hippolytus* (Orange Tree Theatre); *Epsom Downs, The Suicide* (Cockpit Theatre); *Hamlet* (Tivoli, Dublin).

He also writes and produces music for television and very occasionally for fun.

Jon Foster – *Tom*

Theatre includes: *A New Way to Please You, Sejanus: His Fall, Speaking Like Magpies, Thomas More* (Royal Shakespeare Company); *Dr Jekyll and Mr Hyde* (Babayaga Theatre Company); *Free From Sorrow* (Living Pictures); *Romeo and Juliet* (Creation Theatre Company); *Oliver Twist* (Instant Classics); *The Melancholy Hussar* (Etcetera Theatre); *The Two Gentlemen of Verona* (Pentameters Theatre); *Treasure Island* (Palace Theatre).

Television includes: *Silent Witness*.

Christopher Heimann – *Director / Co-Writer*

Christopher is a theatre director, acting teacher and workshop facilitator. Christopher recently directed *Interior* at the Young Vic Theatre in London, as well as directing and co-writing *100* for his company **the**imaginary**body** (Edinburgh Fringe First Award and world tour). Other theatre directing includes *Peer Gynt, Out There* and *Bold Girls*. Christopher teaches acting and improvisation at the Royal Academy of Dramatic Art in London and has run workshops in a wide range of settings including the Big Issue Foundation, Actors Centre London and Brunel University. His work in corporate facilitation includes events around communication, behaviour, creativity and team building, for clients including HM Revenue & Customs and Orange.

Joel Horwood – *Co-Writer*

Joel's first play *Mikey the Pikey* premiered at the Gulbenkian Theatre, Canterbury in 2004. It was selected for the National Student Drama Festival, where Joel won the Cameron Mackintosh Award for Outstanding Contribution to Musical Theatre. The production subsequently enjoyed sell-out performances at the 2005 Edinburgh Fringe Festival. The Stephen Joseph Theatre, Scarborough, commissioned Joel's second play *Cattleprod Shakedown*, which was produced in November 2005.

Joel is a part of the BBC and Royal Court's The 50 scheme and has recently been commissioned by Immediate Theatre to work on the Gascoyne Estate towards a devised piece for the Arcola Theatre, London in September.

Ruth Little – *Dramaturg*

Ruth has been Dramaturg and Artistic Associate at the Young Vic since 2003. Previously she was Literary Manager at Out of Joint, Soho Theatre and Griffin Theatre Company (Sydney), and Senior Reader at the Royal Court.

Shereen Martineau – *Cordelia*

Shereen trained at RADA.

Theatre includes: *The Bacchae of Baghdad* (Abbey Theatre, Dublin); *Tejas Verdes* (Gate Theatre); *Twelfth Night* (Albery Theatre); *Turn of the Screw* (Wolsey Theatre, Ipswich); *Measure for Measure, Richard III, Titus Andronicus* (Royal Shakespeare Company); *Rome and Juliet* (Liverpool Playhouse).

Television includes: *Doctors, TLC, The Last Detective, The Bill, Holby City, EastEnders.*

Graham O'Mara – *George*

Theatre includes: *A Man of Letters* (Orange Tree); *The Three Musketeers* (Young Vic); *Romeo & Juliet* (Wylde Thyme); *Emma* (Good Company); *David Copperfield* (Eastern Angles). Graham is a member of the *Di Trevis Workshop*.

Television includes: *Silent Witness, Casualty, Superfakes, Check Please / Gur.*

Diene Petterle – *Co-Producer*

Diene is primarily a television / film producer and director. Recent credits include Gordon Ramsay's *F Word* for Channel 4, *Hannah Glasse: The First Domestic Goddess* for the BBC (presented by Clarissa Dickson Wright, one of the 2 Fat Ladies), *Europe's Richest People* for ITN and *Page Turners*, presented by Jeremy Vine for the BBC. She has won four international awards as a film director and has had her films screened in Cannes, London International Film Festival, Berlin and many others. *Mr Thompson's Carnation*, one of her films, was theatrically released in cinemas in London. Co-Artistic Director of **the**imaginary**body**, Diene co-wrote and produced *100*.

Ric Watts – *Co-Producer*

As well as *Food*, Ric is currently working on *A Russian Love Tale* with Andrew Bailey (BAC), *Particularly in the Heartland* by The TEAM (Traverse, BAC and UK tour) and *The Baba Yaga* by Mervyn Millar. Until December 2005, Ric was the Producer at Your Imagination, where he developed award-winning new work by Ridiculusmus (*How To Be Funny*), Cartoon de Salvo (*The Chaingang Gang, The Sunflower Plot*), Kazuko Hohki (*Evidence for the Existence of Borrowers*), and Your Imagination (*The Ratcatcher of Hamelin*) for venues as diverse as the Barbican and BAC in London to allotments in Surrey and Nottinghamshire.

Ann Yee – *Movement Director*

Ann trained at The Ohio State University, The Boston Conservatory of Music and Harvard University.

Recent theatre choreography and movement direction includes: *Hamlet, Sweet Charity*: the workshop showing *Hair* (RSC); *The Odyssey, The Magic Carpet* (Lyric Theatre, Hammersmith); *Lysistrata* (Arcola Theatre); *Sex, Chips and Rock & Roll* (Royal Exchange, Manchester); *The Odyssey* (Bristol Old Vic); *Orestes 2.0* (Guildhall School of Music & Drama); *Woyzeck* (Gate Theatre); *Spiderdance* (National Youth Music Theatre); *Evita* (Boston Conservatory of Music). Ann's many awards include a nomination for Best Choreographer for *Hair* for Whatsonstage Awards.

Her contemporary choreography, devising and assisting work includes ongoing research with multi-media and performance collective Fat Annie; *Space* for Barbican YMCA; *All You Can Eat, This, Tag,* and *Prey* for Ohio State University; *In The Between* for Ohio State University, State University of New York, Brockport and University of Maryland.

FOOD

Joel Horwood

Christopher Heimann

theimaginary**body**

Characters

Frank Byrne
Cherry Byrne, *Frank's wife*
George Byrne, *Frank and Cherry's son*
Cordelia Byrne, *Frank and Cherry's daughter*
Tom Smith, *Frank's best friend / sous chef*

Jack Fontaine, *patissier*
Gunn, *kitchen porter*
Brigitte Porte, *gardé manger*
Reggie Le Mains, *patissier*

Peter Longorias, a *food journalist*
Harry Rosen, *a contributing editor*
Sue, *a chat show host*
Brad, *a reporter*
Reporter, *a reporter*

Demart, *head of the Michelin Guide*
Secretary, *Demart's secretary*

Director, *film crew*
Assistant, *film crew*
Clapper, *film crew*

Father, *restaurant customer*
Son, *restaurant customer*

A forward slash (/) in the dialogue indicates that the next character begins speaking at that point.

This text went to press before the end of rehearsals so may differ slightly from the play as performed.

FRANK *is underwater but it's like he's flying, drifting in an underwater breeze. The sounds of water rushing, gurgling and bubbling build to a roar.*

The sound cuts out and FRANK *is on a beach, on a summer's day. He is looking over the sea as he refills a spoon with the last bite of a gooey chocolate thing.*

Cherry
There are moments aren't there? Just moments, everything just melts . . . into . . . perfect happiness . . . Remember that beach . . . In Greece?

Frank (*realising he has missed what she has said*)
Sorry, were you – ?

Cherry (*smiling*)
Never mind.

FRANK *spoons an inky chocolate bite into her mouth.*

OH . . . Amazing . . . Got any more?

Frank
No, I was just . . . experimenting, end of a shift stuff, you know.

Cherry (*kisses him suddenly*)
You are a genius!

Frank
I know I can make this stuff, but I have to follow orders.

Cherry
It's like me – hardly anything I do gets printed. You're still cooking, still creating –

Frank
Yeah, but it's factory work, you make a little piece, you become a little piece. I'm not a machine, I'm – I'm a fucking animal! With these ugly, scarred hands I could –

and it's raw energy but . . . I'm here; ideas coming off me like static and Chef's just recycling old . . . haute cuisine crap.

Beat.

Cherry

If you had your own kitchen, what would you do?

Frank

Get the right crew . . . Get Tom in.

Cherry

Tom?

Frank

He'd do it for me.

Pause.

Cherry

Get a kitchen and do it.

FRANK *laughs*.

I mean it, use the money, get a kitchen, and do it.

Beat.

Frank

Are you serious?

Cherry

Deadly.

Frank

Cherry . . . That's your money.

Cherry

So? I could help out, it'd be good for me too.

Frank

Our restaurant?

Cherry

Yeah.

Frank

You know it's stupid?

Cherry

It's ridiculous.

Frank

Restaurants are not a wise investment –

Cherry

It's a terrible idea.

They start to laugh, exhilarated by the risk.

Frank

You are! You're serious!

Cherry

Yes I am!

Frank

Let's get a kitchen!

Cherry

Let's do it!

A transition to FRANK's family kitchen. FRANK and TOM are going head-to-head over a bowl of soup. It's a showdown. CHERRY is between them, asleep.

Frank

Snails in nettle soup?

Tom

Snails in nettle soup.

Frank

Tom, you were wasted in that kitchen.

Tom

I frequently was.

Frank

Where'd you get the nettles?

Tom

Friend of a friend, bloke called Caspar, hand picks 'em every morning in Dorset. I blanched them in their own dew.

FRANK *draws his spoon, followed closely by* TOM. *They dip them into the soup. Slurp it and chew at each other.*

There is a moment as they allow the flavours to take hold. FRANK *looks initially convinced, then not so convinced.* TOM *is watching him intently.*

Hmmm?

FRANK's *face changes slightly.*

What?

Frank

A little tame . . .

Tom

Tame?

Frank

You used butter.

Tom

A little, for the snails –

FRANK *tuts.*

Only a sliver, I just wiped 'em with it.

CHERRY *stirs, they watch her. They taste again.*

Frank

Amazing, snails in nettle soup, it's like eating a bloody hedge, but then you're left with that soft aftertaste, where you cheated with the butter, and just after . . .

Tom

What?

Frank

Morels . . . (*Beat.*) Did you cut morels today with the same knife?

Tom

I hate you.

CHERRY *wakes up. She takes in the scene, looks at her watch.*

Frank

Menu review.

Beat.

Cherry

But, we're not opening for a month.

Frank

We're staying ahead.

Cherry (*she tastes the soup, her irritation dissolves*)
Mmm – OH! FUCK! That's – wonderful!

Frank

With a few changes, it could be perfect.

Cherry

You should write cookbooks.

Tom

An autobiography!

Frank

After we get the three Michelin stars.

Tom

What's the title?

Frank

Being Frank.

Cherry

We'll live off the royalties – we can move to Greece!
Next to the sea!

Frank

We'll be Greek gods of cuisine!

FRANK *leads* JACK *into The Boiling Pot kitchen. Any movement that takes an actor into proximity with another must be accompanied by calls of 'backs', 'behind' or 'choud'. The kitchen is in preparation for the day's service.*

I hope you've got your coca leaves and amphetamines, Jack, 'cos we forgot how to sleep long ago. We are

culinary guerrillas, these dishes detonate in the mouth.
My right-hand man, sous chef extraordinaire, Tom
Smith!

Gunn

Chef?

FRANK *signs off some delivery notes.*

Jack

Is that the pork?

Tom

Yeah, Blackspot, farmed by a feller used to be a porn
star.

Jack

And you always cook to the same timing or vary it for
size?

Tom

I cut them, I know the sizes.

Jack

Can I / get a look – ?

Tom

Frank, where'd you find this one?

Frank (*guides* JACK *on*)

On starters and veg, our very own queen of cuisine,
Brigitte Porte! I know, she's a girl, swears like a trooper
though.

Gunn

I clean the shit.

Frank

This is your station, desserts, bread . . .

JACK *has deftly set up his mis-en-place in moments.*
FRANK *is amused by* JACK's *adept response. He looks
to* TOM *and smiles before guiding* JACK *on.*

I do the fish, the sauces and the ball-breaking. (*To
everyone.*) Okay, first in at half twelve, thirty for lunch,
and forty for dinner, plus walk-ins.

The printer jerks noisily to life.

Four amuse, two tuna, one asparagus, one scallops.

Gunn *and* **Brigitte**
Oui, Chef.

Frank
Now I keep all this up here. (*Indicates head.*) I know exactly what's happening on each table. Right now, the amuse is arriving on table nine. Our hostess, Sabine, is welcoming the businessmen to table seven in that low-cut top.

The starters arrive.

Service!

Printer fires.

One sea bass, one beef rare, two pork!

Tom *and* **Brigitte**
Oui, Chef!

Frank
I'm moving the orders along – (*Indicates head.*) up here, timing is everything, it's all about rhythm, the sea bass is ready, so Brigitte should have the –

Brigitte (*as she delivers the vegetables*)
Chef.

Frank
And Tom –

Tom (*delivering as a timer goes off*)
The squealer.

Frank
Service! Two amuse, two terrine.

Gunn *and* **Brigitte**
Oui, Chef.

Frank
Three chocolate soufflé, two parfait, two sorbet!

Pause.

Frank (*turns to* JACK)
Three chocolate soufflé, two parfait, two sorbet. If you're not listening you can get out.

Jack
Oui, Chef.

Frank
This is the deep end Jack, it's natural selection.

The printer sound grows rapid, becoming the sound of a machine gun. The kitchen becomes a foxhole in the middle of a battle.

Service! Two bass, three halibut!

All
Oui, Chef.

Frank
Five amuse, two lamb, one medium beef, two pork!

A bomb hits. JACK is separated from the platoon by the blast.

All
Oui, Chef.

Frank
Jack, get the pac-o through the sorbets. Service! The soufflé, Jack?

Jack (*wondering, shell-shocked, through the danger zone*)
Made to order from chocolate we make ourselves, served with malted milk ice cream also made on site, and honeycomb that I made last night while we were working on the bread.

Frank
Let's go, Tom.

TOM *goes to save* JACK.

Gunn, get back on those plates now.

Brigitte (*to* GUNN)
More Tuna.

TOM *has dragged* JACK *back to safety.*

Frank
Three-star work Tom. Service! Four lamb.

Tom
Oui, Chef.

Frank
Halibut's up, Tom, where's the – ?

It's arrived.

Jack
Service!

Frank
I knew you'd fit in. Gunn, we need water.

Gunn
Oui, Chef.

BRIGITTE *is looking through binoculars.*

Brigitte
Chef, Sabine say table twenty is one man with a note
pad.

Frank
Did he drive?

Brigitte
On Michelin tyres.

Printer sounds.

Frank (*laughing*)
Gunn, table twenty gets the beluga. We've got another
inspector in!

All
Oui, Chef.

*A lighting change denotes a transition to a different
time, after a hard service. The staff are exhausted,*

TOM *is cleaning his station,* GUNN *is mopping up, and* BRIGITTE *is asleep on the side.* FRANK, *however, has not broken his stride . . .*

Frank

It's about preparing something that will become a part of someone else, it's community, it's connection, it's primitive communication! When they come to The Boiling Pot, Mr. Fontaine, they walk out discerning eaters, more aware, improved, and yes, more intelligent. Try this, come on, taste . . .

JACK *tastes and, over the following, is moved by the food.*

We manipulate sensation with taste . . .

JACK *just about recovers.*

And aftertaste.

JACK *is suddenly moved again. Beat.*

Jack

That's the best fucking thing I've ever tasted . . . I think . . . I think I might cry . . .

Frank

You're here to learn, Jack, tomorrow you're making that, and when you're ready to move on you'll probably be better than me –

Jack

No, *that* was . . .

Frank

You've got it Mr. Fontaine, the hunger, it's what drives a chef, *experience*!

Jack

Thanks, Chef.

Frank

You have that instinct that even a humble soup, when you really get *into* it . . .

They get into the soup.

. . . you *know* that the opal-coloured lobster that relaxed in the pot, relaxed with a sigh as its old armour loosened, it made this. And when they taste him, they're Jacques Cousteau, Steve Zissou, Ahab riding Moby fucking Dick . . .

The scene changes over the following. FRANK *is in bed with* CHERRY . . .

A hedonist, a voyeur, because food is – FOOD is feeling, food is chewing, food is mawing, gorging, eating, licking, food is touching –

Cherry
Holding –

Frank
Gripping –

Cherry
Tonguing –

Frank
Nourishing –

Cherry
Nibbling –

Frank
Kissing –

Cherry
Loving –

Frank
Loving –

Cherry
Love –

They are breathless in the dark.

Frank
I love it when flavours come together.

Cherry
Mmm?

Frank
I love it when we come together.

After a moment a timer goes off. FRANK *turns on the light and gets out of bed as quietly as possible.*

Cherry
Wh-where . . . ?

Frank
Sh . . . sleep, love.

He helps her back to bed and begins to get dressed. CHERRY *suddenly sits upright.*

Cherry
Uh – time to get up?

Frank
No, Cherry

Cherry
What?

Frank
Not for you.

He gently helps her back into bed.

Cherry
But the – ?

Frank
No.

Beat. CHERRY *lies back down.*

Cherry
Are you getting dressed? (*She checks the clock.*) It's – Frank, ohhhh – it's three in the morning.

Frank
Fish.

Cherry
They're not awake yet.

Frank
I'm gonna catch 'em napping. I'll bring you one back.

Cherry (*sarcastic*)
Brilliant. They're still fresh in an hour, aren't they?

Frank
Not *as* fresh, I'll be back before you know it.

Cherry
Don't wake the kids up.

Frank
Yes, Madam.

He kisses her cheek.

Cherry
Can I have some water, please?

Frank
Yes, Madam.

Cherry
I was just dreaming about Greece . . .

Frank
I've a good feeling today, Michelin can't hold back
forever –

Cherry
It's only been a year.

Frank
Already?

He tucks her in.

Cherry
Go on then. 'Go get 'em.'

Frank
The stars?

Cherry
Fish! You fool! The fish!

*FRANK is already at his place in The Boiling Pot
kitchen during service.*

Frank

Tom, what's this?

Tom

The pureed parsnips –

FRANK *wipes it off.*

Frank

I decided against it. Bardot, ou est l'asperge?

Brigitte

Oui, Chef.

Frank

Tom, you're here because you can get things done. So concentrate on the –

Tom

They love the parsnips.

Frank

Jack, what do you think, serve the beef with the celeriac and cèpes, *and* the parsnip puree?

Jack

Might be a bit much, Chef.

Tom

To the bread man it might be a bit much – Chef, when did this kitchen become a democracy?

Frank

My sentiments exactly, Tom. The parsnip's off. Two terrine, three nettle soup, one asparagus.

Brigitte

Oui, Chef.

A timer starts going off.

Tom

Frank, it *tastes* delicious –

Frank

So does chocolate but only wankers put chocolate sauce with fish! I don't have time for this shit –

Jack

Tom, the lamb . . .

He points.

Tom

Frank, listen –

Frank

In this room, you call me Chef.

Jack

The lamb's – fuck it.

JACK *moves to push into* TOM*'s section.*

Tom

The parsnips work!

Frank

I've fired people for less!

Tom (*steps in* JACK*'s way*)
Where's your section?

Jack

Well if you're fired, it's probably here!

Beat.

Frank

Those soufflés need to go, Jack.

Jack

Oui, Chef.

Frank

Tom, you agreed, that in here –

Tom

I didn't agree to that!

He indicates JACK.

Beat. FRANK *calms* TOM.

Frank

You're my Sundance Kid, Tom, my Robin, my Hutch, my Lacey – Did you fuck that lamb?

Tom

Yeah, fucked it.

Frank

So get another.

Tom

Oui, Chef.

Frank

You're my hero, Tom.

They all resume cooking.

Gunn, more water in here! Brigitte, that tuna should have gone. (*To* JACK, *serious*.) Jack, never leave your station during a service again.

Jack

Chef.

FRANK *is at home.* GEORGE *is ten and* CORDELIA *is twelve.* FRANK *and* GEORGE *are kneading bread.* CORDELIA *is with* CHERRY *working through English homework, whilst* TOM *is reading* Sugar *and eating Coca Cola bottles.*

Frank

The secret's in the texture, feel it George, get your hands into it there, go on . . . It's alive really, you see, it's like it's got a gestation period.

George

Jest . . . ?

Frank

Gestation.

Cordelia

Dad, he's too much of a baby to learn bread.

Cherry

Concentrate, you.

Tom

HAH! Listen, listen, 'My boyfriend says men get a limited number of erections and that if I don't – '

Cherry

Tom!

Beat.

George

Erections –

Frank

George! George, you've got to feed it when it needs yeast or flour.

Beat.

Cherry

It's so much better when you're home.

Cordelia

Mu-um, I thought you were taking us swimming.

Cherry

Later, yes.

Cordelia

But, Dad's gonna be working. (*To* FRANK.) I thought you were gonna come swimming.

Frank

Soon.

FRANK *forces the pace as the scene switches to The Boiling Pot during another prep session.* CHERRY *is hesitant to enter the kitchen. A phone starts ringing.*

How soon?

Tom

The office said the order left the factory an hour ago.

Frank

When it arrives, bollock the driver – we don't deal with slackers.

Cherry

Frank, I don't know how to put it through –

Frank

What?

Cherry

The phone Frank, I can't put it through –

Frank

Don't worry, you've done it, it's done.

Cherry

It's a journalist. Line two, it's flashing.

Frank

Thanks, love. (*Answering*.) Frank.

Harry

Mr. Byrne, my name's Harry Rosen, I was in –

Frank

Pave of cod, beef, chocolate soufflé.

Harry

Yes, yes exactly. Er – I'm calling because I'm recommending The Boiling Pot in the next issue, I've just got a few questions.

Frank

Mm-hmm.

Harry

You've got your first Michelin star in record time . . . ?

Frank

Yes.

Harry

And you're tipped to get a second this year – I have to ask you about the vegetarian options . . . You don't have many.

Frank

No. Why would I? Food broadens experience, it should teach us – not eating oysters? Not eating sweetbreads? I can understand the cruelty argument, well-treated animals taste better, that's fact. But I pity the vegetarians, the real criminals are the ones that won't eat *everything*. It's like opting for celibacy. We're natural omnivores – look at our dental structure, for God's sake, anything goes! Lamb blood, chicken feet, bullock bollocks. The world's animals feed the world's animals. Hugh Fearnley-Whittingstall flambéed a placenta, if I could get a steady enough supply it'd be a fixture on the menu. The survivors of disasters forced to eat other passengers or whatever – they've touched something so primitive, so instinctual . . . I'm jealous! The old Polynesian tribes only ate the bravest of their enemies – give me a few years and I'll have Wayne Rooney on the menu. The same as any of the meat we serve, it's disrespectful not to enjoy it. It just wants a good review.

TOM *walks into the kitchen during prep, holding the published feature and reading the rest of* FRANK*'s quotation.*

Tom

'So, roast my shank slowly, maybe with a little cider and potato stock, let flavours speak for themselves and you've got "long pig" . . . '

TOM *claps* FRANK *on the back.*

They made a bloody feature out of it!

Frank

What's the headline?

Tom

'Dead Meat!'

FRANK *laughs.*

JACK *brings a saucepan over to* FRANK *who can smell it coming.*

Frank

Fig purée?

Jack

Yes, Chef.

Frank (*tastes*)

That's . . . (*He nods.*) That's it Jack. You've got it.

Jack

Thanks, Chef.

Frank

You must have itchy feet by now.

JACK *shifts.*

We said when you got here, that you'd be moving on soon enough, didn't we? (*Beat.*) I made some phone calls.

JACK *looks at the purée, over the following a spotlight on this conversation drops the rest of the kitchen into darkness as all other sounds dwindle.*

Jack

Thank you, Chef.

Frank

We're modern-day beat-poets, me and you, no one's got the reins on us, we keep moving, learning, never staying long enough to get stuck. I was moving for a long time before this, a short trip to the hotel across the valley, then Dublin and then to France, to Bocuse, and Robuchön – that was a lesson. (*Impersonating.*) 'Emmerdeur! Tu as la cervelle qui sort par la queue!'

The Boiling Pot is gearing up as service begins around FRANK.

And all that before London, and Harvey's –

Tom

Don't remind me.

Frank

That was filthy Jack, coke to accelerate, Ketamine to relax –

Tom

Jack?

Frank

What?

Tom

He left, Frank.

FRANK*'s face is blank.*

Jack. He went to Spain.

Frank
Already?

FRANK *finally registers that the scene has changed.*
A printer sounds and the kitchen is in service.

Tom
A while ago . . . You asked me to get someone, and I
got The Hands.

Frank
Reggie The Hands? From Bocuse?

Reg
C'est moi, Chef?

Beat.

Frank
Three soufflé, two sorbet.

Reg
Oui, Chef.

The printer.

Frank
Two amuse and two Tuna.

Gunn *and* **Brigitte**
Oui, Chef.

Frank
Halibut, two beef, rare, medium.

Tom *and* **Brigitte**
Oui, Chef.

Frank
Parfait, two sorbet.

Reg
Oui, Chef.

CORDELIA *arrives with a skinned knee.*

Cordelia
Da-ad?

The pace of the kitchen falters.

Dad, my knee's come off.

Frank

SERVICE! Expedite my daughter to hospital!

TOM removes CORDELIA from the kitchen.

Cordelia

Dad?

The kitchen is almost immediately back to operating smoothly, timers make moments of sound before being touched off, plates are seamlessly handed over as The Boiling Pot gears up for perfection.

Frank

Bass! Soufflé? Lamb. Scallops. Beef. Sorbet. Tuna. Foie gras. Months flicker by in meals and orders.

The staff simultaneously speak their reviews.

Brad

The Connemara grazed, milk-fed / lamb, baked in the hay from its home barn with Irish potatoes and wild truffles seduced me entirely.

Sue

Working his magic at the heat-buckled / oven, the space in Frank Byrne's kitchen, crackles with scalding fat and curses.

Peter

The Boiling Pot is a comet / hurtling through the culinary firmament powered by the extraordinary passion of one young man in a hurry.

Harry

I laughed at the nettle soup / with snails, I cried with delight at the simplicity, the beauty – thank goodness for Frank!

Frank

Everything is making perfect sense. Food that's taken years to seed, feed and culture, is condensed on to the plate. The land speaks a language and here it's focussed into a dialect, into a perfect piece of poetry on the plate.

The staff around FRANK form the image of a Hindu god. The phone rings and all the kitchen staff take up their positions at their respective stations.

Beat.

(*Answering the telephone.*) Boiling Pot. (*Beat.*) Yep. (*Beat.*) Michelin?

The kitchen freezes.

Yes, of course. (*Beat.*) No, not – Yes. (*Beat.*) Thank – Thank you, yes.

FRANK *puts the phone down and the kitchen roars back into full service.*

(*Quietly.*) We've done it. We've DONE IT!

Everyone stops.

THREE STARS!

Everyone reacts in a moment, sounds of fireworks, camera flashes and celebration echo as the reaction freezes. FRANK *watches a raw steak pass, blood spilling off its edge and down the arm of the expediter as it heads for the dining room. His eyes follow the steak and he sits, trembling.*

FRANK *is alone.* TOM *stumbles over drinking cooking brandy and singing 'Starman' by David Bowie.*

Tom (*singing badly*)
HA! Now I know why they have awards, it's so that you can say FUCK YOU, to all them who said . . . (*Swigs.*) You know . . . Remember . . . remember before Paris, with Bocuse – no – Roux – no – anyway. Where we met, you know?

FRANK *nods.*

There. And you – what did you do, he asked you to throw a little more on –

Frank

And I threw you.

Tom

Yeah. Throw a little moron. Boom boom! I fell into the fucking truffle thing though . . . with the – (*Gestures.*) Had to make the dog's meals after that, didn't I? He got some fucking good food too. Fucking good. Fuck 'em though – THREE STARS!

Beat.

Frank

Did you call your parents?

Tom

Yeah. Proud. Crying! Ha! You? Call your dad?

Frank

Yeah . . . he didn't really . . . He knew he *should* be impressed . . . he didn't force it though, you know? Which is good.

Tom

Course he was proud! Three fucking stars! (*He drinks.*) Come on. Let's get back, come on . . . (*Starts singing a bit.*)

Beat.

Frank

What do I do now, Tom? (*Beat.*) What now?

FRANK *stands, and the scene is back to the The Boiling Pot kitchen at a busy time.* GUNN *and* BRIGITTE *arrive, closely followed by* REG.

Gunn (*pointing outside*)
Plates, Chef!

Brigitte

Chef, the plates are smashed –

TOM *arrives, obviously hungover.*

Frank

I chucked the old ones, the new plates will be here in

an hour, traditional handcrafted – Reg, last night I
improved the sorbet, here.

Reg
Last night?

Tom (*uncomfortably aware of others*)
Chef, we only got the three stars last night –

Frank
Are you finding it all a bit tiresome? 'Cos if it's difficult
we should probably stop, shouldn't we? In case we end
up putting ourselves on the line, or taking a bit of
responsibility. (*Change of tactic – to everyone.*) You
should be enjoying the pain – like a boxer. Pain is your
friend, it makes you stronger, so let's get going!

Tom (*clapping*)
Come on, let's go.

Frank
We're heavyweight champions now – we drop our
hands, someone knocks us out.

Tom
Only seventeen hours 'til bedtime.

Frank
We've got a full house booked and I've already got a
hard-on. (*Quietly to TOM.*) Tom, pull a prank or
something will you, I need them laughing.

*A burst of applause as FRANK, led by SUE, is
wrenched into the spotlight of a TV interview.*

Sue
Frank, what a story: three stars in four years!

Frank
It's unbelievable.

Sue
Must be. So what do the stars mean to you?

Frank
Everybody thinks Michelin just pump things full of air,
you know? But these stars, they're like a Nobel prize,

Sue, the crock of gold, you know, they mean that things are perfect.

Sue

With all the hard work, do you have time to see your / family or . . . ?

Frank

Yes, yes I do, my wife, Cherry, has a flair for the PR work, so I see her a lot more now and the children are busy with school so . . .

Sue

Your father's back in Ireland?

Frank

Yes, yes he is.

Sue

And your mother? (*Beat.*) She died during childbirth, didn't she?

Frank (*Nodding*)

Yeah.

Sue

So, was it a lonely childhood, or – ?

Frank

No, no, when Dad was home, we'd go sea fishing and swimming . . . And I was eight or nine and making butter and cheese with the local farmers, helping with the calving, the slaughtering. Have you ever tasted fresh milk, Sue?

Sue

Well . . .

Frank

Milk that's still warm, straight from the udder, I mean, you're basically under there suckling it yourself? After that, cows are little miracle machines, little four-legged factories. So, when Dad was back, getting the fish cooked right, it was language, it was the glue that stuck us together. There's so much joy in watching someone eat something you've created. Perfect.

FRANK *arrives home after the talk show.* GEORGE, *who is reading at the table, notices him.*

George (*looks up*)
Dad?

Frank
What are you doing up?

GEORGE *shrugs.* FRANK *checks his watch.* GEORGE *is looking at* FRANK. FRANK *doesn't know what to say. Beat.*

What are you reading?

George
Oh – er, one of Mum's things in *The Times*, it's a review of the bistro but they talk to Mum in it –

Frank
What does it say?

George
Er . . . It –

Frank
What does she say?

George
Well . . . She's saying how you met – er – 'In his kitchen he is oblivious to the searing heat and the cuts from crabshells and knives.'

Frank
That's not bad.

George
She says, 'The restaurant is like a schizophrenic, just a doorway between the constant murmured compliments of the dining room and the corner of hell where you're the towering god casting judgement and punishment upon your cowed staff.'

Frank
Wow.

George

Sells papers.

Frank

What?

George

Sells papers. I don't know. Mum says it. I don't know what it means.

FRANK *joins the 'soft opening' of Frank's new bistro, Byrne Out. The sound of the hubbub of these occasions fills the room, and* CHERRY *passes him one of the glasses of champagne.*

Cherry

Harry, thank you, so much for this column, it means so much to me –

Harry

This bistro is beautiful – Frank!

Peter

Congratulations, Frank, canny move opening a new spot.

Harry

Great location – Cherry, you know Peter, don't you?

Cherry

Yes, *The Times*?

Peter

Times, Standard . . . So what's the new book called, Frank?

Frank

Food.

Peter

Great.

Harry

Isn't it?

Cherry

Yes.

Peter

I don't know how you do it, Frank.

Frank

Drugs.

Awkward laughs.

FRANK *returns with the same drink to the Boiling Pot kitchen, where he joins* JACK FONTAINE.

Jack

This was all from your idea really, when you were telling me how you got here. They're just documenting me visiting the kitchens and people who inspired me.

Frank

Sounds good, so what do you need me to do?

Jack

Well, when they get here, maybe you could take us through your philosophy, the flavours speaking for themselves stuff, refining the tastes, the freshest produce – that really influenced me.

Frank

Did it?

Jack

Completely. I went straight from Frank Byrne purism to Ferran's laboratory, it was like hot steel into cold water, you know? I knew what I wanted to do pretty much immediately.

Frank

Which is?

Jack

Well the press say it's lab-based but it's –

Frank

Like El Bulli?

Jack

A bit but . . . people are too used to conventional – the world's changing, there's a constant demand for new things; textures, opposites, new combinations – like you said, it's about putting a bomb under all this, about setting something free, that's so right! We'd combine chalk with cheese if the tastes worked, we've got parmesan foam with raspberry muesli, twenty-five courses, it's playful, it's provocative, it's theatre, the menu's rolling, nothing's allowed to be 'a classic' . . .

Frank (*gesturing for calm*)
Parmesan foam with muesli . . . ?

Jack
It's not about specifics, it's about –

Frank
It's all about specifics!

Beat.

Jack
Yesterday we ran a condiment; caramelized olives with sea cucumber wrapped in cuttlefish. Our cooking times are in seconds, Frank.

Frank
You want me on your TV show as the past.

Jack
No –

Frank
This cuisine has evolved Jack, it wasn't scientifically generated, it wasn't – *paf!* There it is, as soon as someone saw a Jersey Royal through a microscope.

Jack
I'm not trying to replace you –

Frank
Humans have been eating since day one, food and our species evolved together –

Jack
This is the next step.

Frank

And I'm the missing link? This food, here. The food here, Jack, the food you helped to develop. Whatever you're talking about is *not* the evolution of it. It's a gimmick, a flash in the pan – Allowing people to taste the perfect fucking tomato will change their lives! They'll know the definition of Tomato! It's not a shrink-wrapped lump, it's a bright red organ, fed with shit and thunderstorms, clawed from the earth with bare, ugly hands, it bleeds and it *tastes*, Jack. You're hiding that –

Jack

Not hiding it.

Frank

You're making it into / something it's not.

Jack

If I treat a tomato a certain way it can end up as a lollypop. It won't be a tomato any more, it'll have a crunchy texture with a refined taste, crystallised into a tingling memory, entirely new.

Frank

And completely fabricated!

Jack

Isn't that what cooking is Frank? Taking mundane materials and making them into something priceless, into an unforgettable experience –

Frank

You went wrong at mundane.

Jack

Shots of taste for courses, no three star stuffiness, just *fun*. Chez Fontaine, they can eat flavoured air.

Frank

They can't eat it –

Jack

Don't you want to try that?

Frank

Can't feel it –

Jack

It's *taste* without complex carbohydrates and saturated
fat –

Both at boiling point.

Frank

Without love!

Jack

For you or your food?

Frank

Is this a fucking bowel movement, Jack!

Jack

YES!

Frank

I am my food! (*Indicating surroundings.*) This food is my
gastric juices, my intestines, my enzymes, my blood red
meat!

Jack

So is mine, Frank.

Frank

You *were* ME! You're getting fat off me now, you're –
You're a tumour!

TOM *enters.*

I'll CUT YOU OUT!

Tom

OI! (*Between them.*) The fuck is this? (*Beat.*) When you
two have stopped flirting, there's a film crew outside.

Jack

I'm not staying.

Frank

Send them in! Bring them in, Tom, we'll do it. For Jack.
Because I'm perverse! I'm a fucking animal and no

science here, no reasoning! You worked here, but don't you dare say you learned.

A DIRECTOR snaps FRANK into the filming of an advert for his 'cooking kits'.

Director
Action!

Frank
Hi, how are you, I'm Frank Byrne, and I'm here to tell you about my new, fun and playful range of cooking kits. They give you the Frank Byrne hit you need for a tenth of the price. You too can have my perfect cuisine without the fear of going to / a three star . . .

Director
Cut!

An assistant mops FRANK's brow, someone with a clapper changes the number of the take.

Frank, I love the improvising, can we just try a take sticking to the script?

Frank
Oh, right.

Director
Everyone?

Frank
Can I get a look at a script then?

Beat. CHERRY brings FRANK a script – he looks over it as everyone resets.

Assistant
Your daughter's on the phone, she says you were supposed to collect her –

Frank
Oh – shit.

He looks to CHERRY.

Director (*clapping with impatience*)
Everyone!

Cherry
Can you organise a cab?

Director
Okay? We'll just keep rolling and cut you up if we need to, positions, and . . .

Clapper
Frank's Food promo, third of August, slate one, take seven.

Clapper sounds and moves out of shot.

Director
Action.

Frank
Hi, I'm Frank Byrne, welcome to The Boiling Pot. We've been working on a new dish for you, tailor-made for your table. It's good honest food, for good honest people, tastefully packaged, and of course, it gets my approval.

FRANK *tastes it and is disgusted.*

Director
Cut! Okay, let's go again, great work Frank, just try to really enjoy it at the end.

The ASSISTANT *comes in and leans over* FRANK *to do his make-up.*

Frank
This – something's . . . How did they cook this?

Director
Still getting a little hard light off that packaging.

Frank
It's in two sections.

Assistant
That's the bit that makes them feel like a chef. They put the red bit in for a minute and the blue bit for two.

Frank

How long ago?

Assistant shrugs.

Director

Positions please.

Frank

Has it been sitting waiting – ? (*To the* DIRECTOR.) When does this go to supermarkets? Is there / time to . . .

Director

It lands in ten days, this is the only day budgeted for, okay – (*Motioning to* CLAPPER LOADER.) Let's go!

Clapper

Frank's Food promo, third of August, slate one, take eight.

CLAPPER *sounds and moves out of shot.* FRANK *looks to* CHERRY *for reassurance.*

Director

Okay . . . Action!

Beat – FRANK *struggles momentarily and then . . .*

Frank

Hi, I'm Frank Byrne, welcome to The Boiling Pot. We've been working on a new dish for you, tailor-made for your table. It's good honest food, for good honest people, tastefully packaged, and of course, it gets my approval.

He tastes it and acts delighted.

Director

Perfect! Frank, you're a genius.

FRANK *changes the scene by offering a group of reporters a plate of dessert samples. It is late afternoon, after a phenomenal meal to launch the new menu.*

Variously

Oh – I thought I couldn't eat any more but –
This is delicious.

This is so good.
Oh, that's – mmm . . .

Peter

Frank, what inspired this season's menu?

Reporter (*with a camera*)

Frank, sorry Frank, could you just stand behind the worktop?

FRANK *moves to behind the worktop.*

Frank

Good?

Reporter

That's great.

Frank

Each element is an explosion of taste! It's fresh, it's irreproachable, I may as well be carving slices off my provider's arses. Everything tastes exactly of itself. You order lamb, you get perfection, baked in the hay from its barn, no vulgar sauces, no stupid sides. This menu redefines taste, with this menu we're selling dreams!

Peter

Frank, your ready-meals landed in shops last week –

Frank

The Cooking Kits?

Peter

Can you tell us about them?

Frank

Sure, we're still perfecting them – everyone should be able to eat great food, every day. Great food makes great families, and this is my attempt at bringing Frank Byrne to everyone.

Laughs.

Brad

And how long can you keep this up?

Beat.

Frank

Hmm?

Brad

How long do think you can you keep this up?

Frank

Keep what up?

Brad

The cooking, writing, the three stars, the appearances −

Frank

You mean, how long can I keep three stars?

Brad

Well, yeah, but I meant −

Frank

What kind of a question is that?

Brad

Er − it's −

Frank

A stupid one? What's your name?

Brad

My name?

Frank

You come here, into my home, my kitchen, eat my food, my words.

Brad

What?

Frank

Is that it? I've got three stars! What have you heard? What are you lot saying to each other?

Brad

Okay, I'm sorry. Maybe I phrased it the wrong . . .

There is an awkward silence. One of the reporters passes the plate with desserts to the others.

Harry

These are so good.

Peter

This is really lovely, Frank.

FRANK *goes to a work surface and simply begins to work.*

The Boiling Pot in prep forms around FRANK. *Everyone knows exactly what they are doing and are completely on top of everything, and in moments they have finished. There is a beat as they relax in what is usually the calm before the storm.*

Frank

Tom? Where's that first booking?

He calls front of house.

Tom

They'll be here, it's only just twenty-past.

Frank (*talking into the phone*)

Did they call to say they'd be late?

He puts the phone down. Beat. FRANK *enters the walk-in alone.*

After a moment TOM *joins* FRANK *in the walk-in.*

Tom

Frank? What are you doing in here? Come on.

Frank

Tom, you're not going anywhere, are you?

Tom

What?

Frank

Don't leave me.

Tom

Leave ya?

Frank

If I lose this star, don't leave me.

Tom

Frank, I'm not going anywhere, mate –

Frank

You would tell me.

Beat.

Tom

Yeah, we've got three stars.

FRANK *is beating his fist.*

Frank

And we've got a full house. We're fully booked for the next four weeks.

Tom

Rave reviews.

Frank

Rave reviews. Three stars. Talk of the town.

Tom (*trying to stop* FRANK *beating himself*)
Frank – stop it. Come on. Frank?

TOM *attempts to stop* FRANK. REG *walks in. He pauses for a moment, registering that* TOM *looks like he's holding* FRANK's *hand.*

Reg

Egg whites.

Steps over them to get the egg whites and exits. TOM *gets up.*

Tom (*beat*)
Okay?

Frank

Okay.

Tom

All right.

FRANK *bursts out of the freezer into the kitchen. We are left with* TOM *alone in the walk in.*

Frank

OKAY! What are you all gawping like you're out of water for, can't a man take a break? I'll do these three halibut, one bass. Gunn help me dress these plates, let's give them something amazing today, let's change their fucking lives, four beef, two lamb, one veal!

Tom (*with vigour*)

OUI, CHEF!

The scene changes to Michelin HQ. DEMART sits at an office desk, he pauses a moment, opens a drawer, reaches into it, takes out a little toy car, a red VW bus. He puts it on the table, winds up its mechanism and lets it run . . . He toys dangerously with it, allowing it to run close to the edge. A sudden knock and his SECRETARY comes in.

Secretary

Sir, excuse –

DEMART *covers the car with his hand.*

Demart

I said I was not to be interrupted this afternoon?

Secretary

It's Frank Byrne for you.

Beat.

Demart (*sighs*)

Put him through –

Secretary

No, he's – he's here sir –

Demart

Here?

Secretary

With his wife, they say it's urgent.

FRANK *bursts into the room, tightly gripping a hat, followed by* CHERRY.

Frank

Hello Sir! You look well, really well, really, thanks so
much for seeing me, thank you, it means a lot, at this
short notice –

Demart

Okay, okay Frank.

Frank

Thank you. H – How are you?

Demart

I'm fine –

Frank

Good. Oh – this is Cherry – Cherry, this is Mr Demart,
also known as The Michelin Man, head of the little red
book, the man behind the scenes of exquisite cuisine –
he's –

Cherry

How do you do?

Demart

We've met before, haven't we?

Cherry

Yes, we have, sorry to spring ourselves upon you / like
this.

Demart

Oh . . . It's fine –

Frank

It was me, I'm sorry, I dragged her here and you away
from . . . Thanks for seeing us.

Demart

Take a seat, please.

They sit. Then DEMART *sits.*

Frank

Yes, yes, oh and – I'm fine yes. Busy, busy as always.
Still a lot of mouths to feed, interviews and things and
the kids.

Demart

I see.

Frank

And you?

Demart

I think you asked me that already. (*Beat.*) I'm fine.
(*Beat.*) I enjoyed reading your most recent cookbook,
very amusing.

Frank

Oh, good, good. Thank you. I . . . Oh, and I think you
were right to give young Jack Fontaine his second star
last year, he's, you know, he's top notch –

Demart

He's very exciting, isn't he?

Frank

He used to be my apprentice, you know?

Demart

Yes, I saw the program.

FRANK *nods.*

Is there anything I can do for you Frank?

Frank

It . . . It's . . . I don't want to bother you really but
it's . . . I'm wondering if you're planning . . . many
changes to the current state of things . . .

Cherry

I'm sorry, Frank's a little agitated, he gets nervous about
meeting you. He holds you in very high regard, he's a
big fan. He, well, we consider it an honour to hold this
third star, it's come to form the foundation of our
business, but above all he's proud to be one of the few
individuals honoured with the three stars.

Frank

Yes, yeah, yes.

Cherry

Of course, being so proud of this achievement he's attempted to maintain his high levels and I think it's fair to say he's concerned about the upcoming publication of this year's Michelin guide. Is that right, Frank?

Frank

Yes, yeah it is, and – Sir? I was wondering if you were planning on taking my star from me.

Demart

Oh.

Frank

Don't.

Demart

Don't take your –

Frank

Don't take it.

Cherry

Frank.

Beat.

Demart

Frank, you know I can't discuss the upcoming publication, these conversations just don't happen. I'm sorry Cherry, but we're very strict here, we can't divulge to *anyone* our intentions / prior to printing.

Frank

I know –

Demart

I mean, if everyone could come in and barter for their stars where would we be? Bedlam. That's where. There'd be no rigour. No frame of reference. People would be confused. (*Beat.*) Frank, I've known you for a long time . . . My hands are tied with this . . .

Cherry

We understand completely, I think part of our visit is just to say thank you as much as –

Frank

Couldn't you at least warn me?

Demart

Warn – My dear chap, I can't say anything.

Cherry

Frank . . .

Frank

I'm sorry – I just mean, as a – as a friend. If you are going to, please, just give me a call, I don't know . . . Say it in code –

Demart

Frank, you certainly don't need a warning. You've risen from an unknown little restaurant, with a cramped kitchen to three stars in . . . in four years? You've had an immense impact on cuisine! I can't say any more. (*Beat.*) Not many chefs have done that, you know?

Frank

I know.

Demart

You've always astounded me with your dedication, your diligence. You should be proud of what you've done, Frank . . .

Frank

Yes, Sir.

Demart

Everything you've achieved so far.

Pause.

CHERRY *and* FRANK *get up and walk towards the door.*

DEMART *leaps onto the table.*

Of course, there is one way you can be certain of it.

Frank

Sorry?

Demart

There is . . . (*He turns away.*) No.

Frank

Go on!? Name it!

Demart

I'm not sure you want it enough –

Frank

I've been working – working night and day – I can't sleep!

Demart

Well, you're twisting my arm here, but, I have always been amazed by what you can rustle up at the drop of a hat.

Frank

Thanks.

FRANK *drops his hat.*

Demart

Ooops! What a coincidence!

DEMART *turns around and is helped off the table by FRANK and CHERRY. He sits down at the top of the table. CHERRY puts a napkin around his neck.*

Frank

W – What would you like sir?

DEMART *points at an empty space.*

FRANK *dashes to open a cupboard – it's empty.*

I'm afraid we've run out of the calf's liver, can I offer you the braised oxtail with wilted brussel sprouts and –

DEMART *points at an empty space.*

FRANK *dashes to open another cupboard – also empty.*

I'm sorry sir, the lamb is off too . . . it's – can't you see it's not there . . . Can I give you something else, some –

DEMART *points at* CHERRY.

Cherry (*flattered*)
Oh! Why thank you –

Frank
This is about me! The stars! Don't bring her into it –

DEMART *points at* FRANK'*s arm.*

FRANK *sees where* DEMART *is looking.* CHERRY *brings a knife.*

Right . . .

FRANK *takes the knife and slowly carves a slice of flesh from his arm. Parallel,* CORDELIA *slices the skin off a cucumber.* FRANK *sinks down on his chair.*

Back at the home, around the table.

Cordelia
Has George told you about his girlfriend yet?

George
She's not my girlfriend.

Cordelia
Her name's Peaches.

George
Well, Cordelia wants to get a tattoo.

Cherry
Well, that's not legal, so . . .

They sit to eat.

George
What did you see in Paris?

Cherry
We went to the Michelin HQ.

George
OOhhh. (*He gestures worship.*)

Cherry

Mr Demart admires your father – I know you say
differently, Frank, but it was obvious! Really. He said
way more than he wanted to when we walked in, he's
fond of you.

George

Can I have some of that – ?

Frank

Help your fucking self.

Cherry

Frank? He's exhausted, ignore him George, of course you
can start. Cordelia, come and sit.

Beat.

Frank

You're acting as if nothing's happened. You know as well
as I do, the papers are gonna have a fucking carnival.

Cherry

Frank, calm down.

Frank

We'll hear every TV set laughing at us, we'll all be
ridiculous, there's gonna be all kinds of – of headlines
and –

Cherry

He admired your diligence.

Frank

As good as a fucking attendance award!

Cherry

All right, all right Frank, if you want to do it like this –
you've had an immense impact / on cuisine.

Frank

Past tense –

Cherry

You should be proud of what you've done –

Frank

Past tense!

Cherry

Frank, he was saying there was no way you'd –

Frank

'My hands are tied Frank.'

Cherry

No way they would –

Frank

I asked him to tell me in code – Give me a warning, I said, be humane, give me a warning –

Cherry

And he called you a friend –

Frank

He said he couldn't –

Cherry

He said –

Frank

'Frank, I can't tell you!'

GEORGE, *who has been quietly playing with his food, stands and exits.*

Cherry

Frank, I was there –

Frank

You weren't listening.

FRANK *is left alone at the table, isolated by the lights. He makes a phone call.* JACK FONTAINE, *who is in his own kitchen experimenting, answers.*

Jack

Hello?

Frank

Jack?

Jack

Frank . . . (*He stops, surprised*.) How's things, how have you – ?

Frank

Fine, yeah, great, I went to see Demart today.

Jack

Michelin?

Frank

Yeah. Listen, have you heard anything?

Jack

What about, Frank?

Frank

About me, from your cooks or . . . I don't know. Maybe someone's said something.

JACK carries on speaking but FRANK has moved on, he has turned slightly and is on the phone to HARRY, the magazine editor.

Harry

Mm-hmm?

Frank

Harry? It's Frank, Frank Byrne –

Harry

FRANK!

Frank

I need to ask you something.

Harry

It's production week, I'm up to my tits in shit, but you're probably / going to ask anyway –

Frank

Do you think I'm boring?

Harry

Boring! Who said what, Frank?

Frank

Demart said he couldn't warn me.

Harry

Michelin Demart?

Frank

He says his hands are tied.

Harry

Demart said this?

HARRY continues to speak in silence whilst FRANK, who has lost interest, dials PETER, who is very sleepy.

PETER makes bear-like sounds of a half-awake singleton.

Frank

Peter? It's Frank. I know it's late, sorry, I just – I spoke to Demart.

Peter

Who?

Frank

Michelin, Demart, Paris. Whatever you've heard, there's blood in the water, I'm sure of it.

Lights fade on FRANK. He lets the phone slip but the phone conversations continue.

Harry

Demart said he was going to lose it?

Peter

He sounded terrified.

Jack

I don't believe it.

GEORGE and CORDELIA are watching TV in their home.

George

So what does this one do?

Cordelia

He's a surfer.

George

And you're gonna move in with him?

Cordelia

Yeah.

FRANK *comes in.*

George

Dad!

FRANK *roughly pulls out the cardboard tube at the centre of a toilet roll and throws it so that it unravels at them. They laugh.*

Frank

You want to live like fucking animals?

Cordelia

Dad?

Frank (*as he roughly destroys and throws a second and third roll*)
When. The. Toilet roll is finished you replace it!

George

Dad! What –

Cordelia

Fuck! DAD!

FRANK *exits.*

GEORGE *sighs and starts to tidy up.*

Leave it. He made it.

George

Well, I should've replaced it so . . .

Cordelia

He's a dick.

She is texting. Beat.

George

It's just how he does things.

Cordelia

Well, it's not normal. I'm gonna go tonight. It won't make a difference.

George

Now?

Cordelia

I'm packed so – yeah, why not?

Beat.

George

How long are you going for?

Cordelia (*she starts helping to tidy up*)

I don't know . . . I'm gonna stay away as long as I can. Cornwall first, then we were talking about driving around France. Maybe going round to Egypt, I think you can drive there, through Greece and Turkey and stuff. I want to see those pyramids and that sphinx before someone blows it up or something. I'll send you postcards if you want.

George

Yeah.

Cordelia

Yeah. Okay, see you Grubby.

George

Yeah. Look, don't call me that in front of Peaches, yeah?

Cordelia

Promise.

She starts to leave.

George

Oh – I've got a Twix . . . (*Offers it.*) Just if you want one. There's a Twix . . .

Cordelia

Can't eat it, exploitation.

George

Oh, forgot.

He throws it in the bin – cheers the shot.

She leaves.

Deli? Send a postcard, yeah? I could do with a postcard
with . . . With things like this . . .

Cordelia

Yeah, bye.

CORDELIA *enters the kitchen with her bags, and
discovers* FRANK *working feverishly.* CORDELIA *pulls
out a cigarette and strikes a match.* FRANK *freezes at
the sound and turns to her. They watch each other, the
threat of smoking in the kitchen is apparent. The
match burns* CORDELIA's *fingers and she waves it out.
He passes her the damp cloth for her fingers.*

I'm leaving . . . Gonna go to Cornwall, with Tyson.

Beat.

Frank

Tyson?

Cordelia

In his van. I told Mum earlier so . . .

Beat.

Frank

When?

Cordelia (*looking at her watch*)

Half an hour.

Frank

No, when did you meet him?

Beat.

Cordelia

We want to start a family, I've always wanted kids
before I'm too old to enjoy it, so . . .

Frank

But you're . . . eighteen.

Beat.

Cordelia

Bye, Dad.

FRANK *is smelling the air in the kitchen.* TOM *joins him.*

Frank (*noticing* TOM *watching him*)

It stinks, something's rotting. (*Briefly carries on.*) Can you smell that?

Tom

No.

Frank

It stinks Tom, the whole place . . . stinks. (*He continues scrubbing – stops suddenly.*) Didn't I always say it has to be fresh – didn't I always say it has to be alive?

Tom

You do, yeah.

Frank

Didn't I? (*Starts scrubbing again.*) Can you not smell it? Is it me, do you think?

Tom

No, Frank, you're just –

Frank

What? Losing it? I'm just what?

Tom

You're not losing anything.

Frank

Well, the Great British Media think differently, Tom. (*Takes crumpled feature from pocket.*) 'Frank Byrne's going to have his work cut out to combat rumours that he is losing his touch – ' Here. (*Throws it at* TOM.) That was Peter! That was Peter, and he's a *friend*!

Beat.

Tom

That's not what it says.

Frank

Read between the lines Tom, it's obvious! That nettle soup's the most popular thing we run, that was your idea.

Tom

Our idea, Frank –

Frank

It's a nice place, Tom. I can see why you'd want it, you want to be the chef, don't you? You reckon you're owed a bite of the Cherry, Tom, don't you? (*Beat – resumes scrubbing.*) It really stinks, it's –

Tom

What posters does George have on his wall? What A-levels is Cordelia doing, Frank? Did you even know she was – ?

Frank

Yes I did!

Tom

You knew that?

Frank

Yes.

Tom

What are they?

Frank

You've got no place in my family! I've seen how you talk to my kids, MY KIDS!

Tom

Bra-fucking-vo. Sharpest knife in the drawer, you just stuck it in, didn't you? Since that phone call, when you got me out of that same fucking kitchen, out of that dead end . . . I mean, completely stuck and I'd started – things were getting out of hand, you know, and then you called . . . Since I got here, since the way we were with

that first menu, I knew I wanted to be a part of this . . .
I wanted us to make our kitchen . . . our food, Frank,
'cos you've got something . . . with people – what you
do to people around you. But you're losing them.

Beat – FRANK *is sorry.*

Everything I've had comes apart in my hands like . . .
mince . . . But not this. Without this, I'm alone, and
that scares me. Okay? That scares the shit out of me.

Beat.

I'm a part of something here, an important part of
something, not just a kitchen, a family . . . I need you to
keep this under control a bit, mate, 'cos I'm shitting
myself. All right? I'm shitting myself.

Frank

Okay.

Tom

Is it?

Beat.

Frank

Yeah. Yeah.

Beat.

Tom

You're still gonna tell me it stinks though, aren't you?

Frank (*starting to scrub slowly*)

It does a bit.

Beat.

Tom

Okay. (*Picks up scrubbing materials.*) Whereabouts?

FRANK's *scrubbing becomes a relevant but reduced
movement of scrubbing at a stain on his clothes in his
bedroom.* TOM *has left and* CHERRY *watches* FRANK
for a moment. He looks up when CHERRY *speaks and
realises he is in his family home. He alters his
behaviour accordingly.*

Cherry
Was this place . . . ? It was supposed to be a launch pad to be – to be a . . . (*Beat.*) Has it gone wrong?

Beat.

Frank
Maybe we should . . . Should we have a holiday?

Cherry
That could be nice.

Frank
A few days or so, in a week or two?

Cherry
Next week is the Guide publication but there's the week after? Oh – I need to get on top of that feature, how about this weekend? Just Sunday and Monday or . . .

Frank
It's Abramovich's birthday thing on Sunday . . . In three weeks or so?

Cherry (*getting ready for bed*)
Let's talk about it closer to the time. (*Beat.*) Are we okay?

Frank
Yeah.

Lights down.

We are in the kitchen during service, but it takes FRANK *a moment to catch up.*

Reg
Service!

Frank
Tuna, halibut, beef.

All
Oui, Chef.

A phone rings, the action continues. FRANK *watches the phone. He reaches for it. Stops. Reaches again and answers.* DEMART *speaks.*

Demart's Voice

Frank, this feels like an annual phone call. As usual, The Boiling Pot has three Michelin stars. Congratulations.

FRANK *smiles a little. Puts the phone down. Walks slowly through his impeccably efficient kitchen. Gradually the staff peel away to leave* FRANK, *alone.* CHERRY *comes in holding a glass of wine.*

Cherry

Love?

Frank

Okay.

The Boiling Pot kitchen morphs around FRANK. *It is the end of service and all are cleaning up. The printer fires. The first four lines are a simultaneous reaction.*

Reg

Sabine!

Tom

Every time!

Brigitte

Merde!

Gunn

I kill them!

Frank (*to* TOM)

It's only a pair. Tom, I do these in my sleep.

Why don't you take everyone for a meal somewhere, on me?

Tom

I'll wait with you.

Frank

No, go on, keeps me on my toes. Everyone? I'm going to take care of this.

Everyone looks at TOM.

Tom
You heard him! Let's go!

Reg
You remember the thing, with –

Frank
Get out.

Beat. FRANK *has the chit in his hand,* TOM *hasn't left.*

Tom
Good to have you back, Frank.

They smile together and TOM *exits, leaving* FRANK *alone.*

Frank (*responding to the order*)
Lobster . . . taking its life into its flesh, when it hits the water, its cold blood skyrockets, it's a rush. And in that rush it remembers everything at once . . . Your lobster . . .

FRANK *is bringing two plates to the two diners, who respond with delight upon seeing him.*

Father
Ah . . . lovely –

Son
We didn't expect this!

Father
Are you the chef?

Son
Dad, this is Frank Byrne, he's a master chef.

Father
He shouldn't be serving us, should he?

Son
Thank you.

He watches for a moment as they are amazed by the taste, then he is suddenly back to work in the kitchen.

Frank

Their soufflé is rising perfectly, I'll leave a cherry at the side. But I'll serve it a little late, let it fall just a touch. They'll only notice it's in trouble if they really look, only if they imagine some tiny improvement . . .

CORDELIA *steps into the kitchen with her bags. She has been crying. FRANK sees her. A moment passes.*

CORDELIA *drops her bags.*

FRANK *runs a blow torch over a crème and passes one to her.*

CORDELIA *accepts it and sits on the side.*

FRANK *passes her a spoon.*

Cordelia

Do you remember when I cut my knee?

Beat.

I did it on purpose, I didn't mean it to be that bad but, I saw the bottle as I fell and . . . You sent me off with Tom.

Pause.

Frank

Did you get a tattoo?

Cordelia

The Simpsons.

Beat.

Frank

All of them?

Beat.

Cordelia nods.

Where?

Cordelia (*indicates in the general direction of her back*)
On the couch.

A crash and GEORGE *arrives. The location should be
confused between the domestic and professional
kitchens.*

George (*slurring and a little clumsy in moving to the toaster*)
Ah, hello. Cordilila! Hello!

Cordelia (*smiles at him*)
Grubby.

George
I'm going to make some toast, to celebrate! Cordelia's
back! You want some toast, Dad? (*He smiles – moved.*)
I know it's late but I haven't been drinking, I swear, why
would I? I've got my whole life ahead of me. (GEORGE
is focusing on putting the toast in.) Toast then.

Beat.

Frank
Is this what you do then? When you're –

George
Hang on, I'm not drunk . . . There was a bit of cider but
cider doesn't get you drunk unless you're a lightweight
and I'm not a lightweight. Not 'cos I drink all the time,
'cos I don't.

Frank
That's good 'cos you're fifteen.

George
Exactly! I've got my whole life . . . You'll like this toast,
it's good bread, I made it. What do you want on it?

Frank
Whatever you're having.

GEORGE *nods and butters the toast.*

George
And don't you fret, you're getting some too.

Cordelia
I didn't say anything.

George

First time for everything.

Cordelia

You've got clever in your old age.

GEORGE *brings the toast over.*

Frank

Just butter?

George

Best way.

They share the toast.

FRANK *turns a light on. He is sitting on the bed with* CHERRY *next to him.* CHERRY *rolls and lays a hand on him. She takes his keys.*

Frank

Fish.

CHERRY *lies back as* FRANK *continues to get dressed.*

Cherry

I was dreaming about . . .

Beat.

Frank

Have you seen my keys?

CHERRY *is holding them.*

Cherry

The dent on your side is shallower, feel, hardly an imprint . . . (*She guides his hand.*) Do you feel that? Feel the difference . . . (*Guides his hand to the dent beneath her. Beat. She kisses him, he kisses her but then stops. Beat.*)

Frank

I'll leave you breakfast.

Beat.

Cordelia came home last night.

CHERRY *is sleepily delighted.*

I love you.

Cherry
'Go get 'em.'

Frank
The fish?

Cherry (*sleepy*)
The stars you fool, the stars . . .

Frank (*tucking her in and kissing her head. He takes the keys from her sleeping hand*)
Night, night.

FRANK *is in the kitchen. He hangs the knives, folds the aprons, makes sure that everything is completely in order, and then picks up his keys and turns off the lights.*

FRANK *walks into the water.*

A Nick Hern Book

Food first published in Great Britain in 2006 as a
paperback original by Nick Hern Books Limited,
14 Larden Road, London W3 7ST, in association with
theimaginary**body** (www.theimaginarybody.co.uk)

Cover image by David Hardcastle, Rubbaglove

Typeset by Country Setting, Kingsdown, Kent CT14 8ES
Printed and bound in Great Britain by Biddles, King's Lynn

A CIP catalogue record for this book is available from
the British Library

ISBN-10   1 85459 955 0
ISBN-13   978 1 85459 955 1